Return to the Mothership

Joanne Kelly

BookLeaf Publishing

Illustrated by Rachel Pearl Millington

Presentation by *BookLeaf Publishing*

Web: www.bookleafpub.com

E-mail: info@bookleafpub.com

ISBN: 9789357210577

First edition 2022

DEDICATION

Dedicated to my parents for all of the love and support they give. I will be forever thankful. And, for my boys George and Charlie the loves and light of my life.

ACKNOWLEDGEMENT

Firstly, I would like to whole-heartedly acknowledge my partner of 18 years for his support and love. Without him- warts and all- I would not have been encouraged to pull together this collection. In addition, my friends and family which have listened to me, counselled me, encouraged and supported me through difficult times. Without you, I might not be standing as tall as I am today. You know who you all are.

Likewise, I thank the teachers and staff of the schools I have worked in whilst working through my moments of darkness. Supporting me whilst I got my mojo back has been much appreciated over the past years.

Please let me also take the time to thank the nurses, doctors and therapists who have helped me to gain insight into how to support my own mental health: some through a lot of medication, and others with advice and guidance.

And perhaps, oddly, I will give thanks to the friends and loves which might not be in my life now. Without knowing it, you also have shaped me into to who I am today, and for that I am thankful.

Lastly, I will acknowledge and thank my two beautifully, wonderful children. My boys. Know this: without you, life would be cleaner and less frantic, but my heart would be lost without you both.

PREFACE

In the depths of lockdown in 2020 I started writing poetry.
1- to try and get out all of my racing thoughts in a new form, other than lists.
2- because I needed to be creative in a new way; I had already painted most things in sight.
3- because it was my way to express hidden emotion, whilst I navigated through a deep depression and the aftermath of some of my darkest days.

Poems are quite like reading lyrics to songs (which I love to read). Knowing music fills my soul, poetry is my way to connect with myself and expel emotion which I can't always get out with tears, screaming and chocolate binges.

Earth Landing

November, 1983
the official paper says we met.
But when I think closely about how this began,
now a mother myself,
I realise:
No stalk came around with a bundle of joy.
No twinkle in my dad's eye.

It didn't start with the pushing and hospital
visits,
nor screams, blood and the fears, and tears.
Dad pacing the corridor and taking breaks to
smoke.
Not the stretch marks which evidence
an invisible thread.
Nor the bundle of joy sleeping at the end
of your bed.

Nor did it start with those sleepless nights,
cracked, bleeding sore nipples,
frazzled mind,
being skint,
one night of passion to bind...

We met in your day-dreams and play time with dolls,
mums and dads games,
plastic dolls you'd dress and adore.
You'd love them and wrap them and feed them with love.
You'd look in their eyes, smile and pray to God above.
A dream of a baby you would love and adore-
a yearning to rock them, all swaddled up tight.
Their silent, yet deafening cries, mimicked my call.

Our adventure was set.

You,
made a wish,
said a prayer,
and an angel heard you.
They knew you were ready to share:
love and the guidance from the soul.
Then along came me.
And this love carried on:
forever.

Ensnared,
always there:
it never goes away.

And now, after those terrible teen years,
screams and slams of doors,
and drinking until dawn.
You still worry now,
I know this.

But, it's still there-
it will never dissipate,
for you are with me always,
and I,
with you.

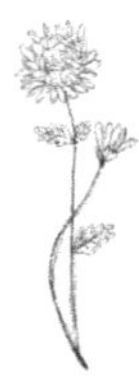

Crabs on the Loose

I didn't feel quite right all day today.
Like I'd lost my keys, again.
And then the date BOOMED loudly inside my mind.
I had forgotten your birthday.
How are you 40?

Flooding my mind and heart-
how can I not sit and muse our special childhood
memories,
when every day was summer.

Running through the fields one summer,
Probably,
definitely, other summers too,
they all merge into one hazy,
bitter tasting memory of times gone,
long gone now.

Healthy, happy, without a care in the world.

In the fields that day we had one aim:
to find the rabbits we had spied through the curtains
of the caravan.

And another day, maybe the same day,
such vivid memories - scratches on our knees and
arms-
climbing trees wasn't just for boys.

Picking plums as our dads looked on.
You the climber for our stolen delights.
And me, the catcher; the look out.
Not sure we helped them catch many fish,
laughing and prattling around.

Maybe you are still up high, watching?
And I wait to catch a sighting when you visit.

And the café – you can't have forgotten that day!
Crabs we had caught running wild on the floor and we,
two dirty, sandy, sunburnt kids scampering around underneath
the tables in our hidden world: cancer free.

Maybe we will get to ride our matching bikes Father Christmas bought us that year again?
And, if only our teletext star signs could have told us those rides,
times,
lives,
wouldn't last.

But – what lasts forever?
Your laugh? Songs we sang?
Or the time I held your baby for the first time?
Dance routines flood my heart as the Carpenters play on Magic FM,
I sob and still think of you.

The last time I saw him- your baby- he stood proud,
smart in a suit,
a big boy now, still sobbing like the babe in arms I
met all those years back.
Daring to stand and attend and applaud,
we stood at your last gig
in the overfilled, large chapel.

Roses were placed on your white coffin, like a stage
filled with ripples of love for a famous, Earth angel.
Your songs filled the room.
Our futile hope of an encore never amounted.

No more fighting.
No more pain.
No more larking out to play hairdressers.

And today, and tomorrow, and yesterday,
we think of you,
like I know you think of us too.

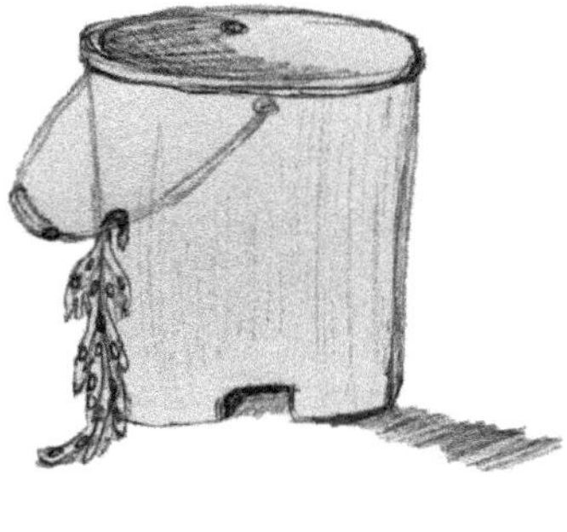

Filthy Fireworks and Fog

The sky was filled with fireworks.
Like my heart they were loud, vibrant:
rage awaiting to escape all over the world.
A celebration- it felt- to take you out of our bunker.
Three days bunkered down,
drugged up to the eyeballs and
surrounded by all the other wounded souls:
warriors awaiting to troop on into the mothering
world far beyond.
Modern day bedraggled Nightingales flew to our
rescue,
when they could.
No breaks, shit pay and knackered.
Yet still, a love-filled warmth radiated from them.

And into this world we fled.
You, me, your comrade and daddy.
This world, and all of it's weird ways.
Even my mind couldn't fathom what had happened…
Lack of sleep.
Pain.
Thick scar tissue, bitterly festered away under
bloody gauze, unbeknown to me-
Just like the poison filling my frazzled mind.

Flashbacks, unlike fireworks, really
never fully fade away, you know.

Blood, weighed at the side on bits of cloth.
What a sight to behold!
I didn't even want him there after the last exposure of dirty truths.
But I saw the texts, which now recline in my fog filled mind and
in his eyes.

Another blast of a flashback:
birth trauma, scared witless and crying for my mum,
hoping, praying I didn't die that night.
Maybe a crushed pelvis- or broken heart- not sure which would have been worse?
Shitting myself after the pain relief.

It's a messy, pleasant sort of thing: birthing a human.

And then, our ten pound blond babe was held over the curtain.
The pain in my heart dissolved as I threw up from the drugs:
irreversible, unforgettable adoration.
He definitely looked like the milkman's: I still use that joke.

Home.
Babe in crib.
And I, high on love, tramadol, fatigue.
Like a WW1 solider battling through the thick shit you created.
Battle wounds congesting: heart, mind, soul.

Raw cuts sewn crudely together and-
rage, held uncomfortably inside, just enough
to emit some
love for our precious babes.

Almost five years on.
Tramadol gone.
Still searching for the why and how I trooped on.
So long.

And those fireworks…
Still ignite.
Lighting the way through the fog,
a search light, interrogating, suffocating,
revealing:
the truth.
And them.
And us.

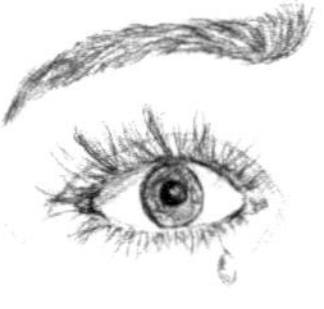

Roulette

To die is the end, but what about the win?
The laughs and the cries, all just fit in.
A tirade of nostalgia- regurgitating
moving back, to transcend,
red-herrings galore…
And the cross roads of danger-
taking comrades as we go.
We u-turn.
We shimmy through the joy and the haze.
Rock through the anger,
Cha cha through pain.
Meander through days,
          sometimes weeks
we're caught off guard,   off kilter.
Slightly, oddly,   off tangent,
but,
then surrender, to: peace.

In sadness we grow;
some happy days may fade.
But to live each day in the now,
is the aim of my game.
Not to win, but to play
roulette.
what's to come?
and the love and the loss
all tangled in one.

How would a day turn into a week,
a month or a year without making mistakes?
Feeling frail, fear and meek.
I hide under duvets and peak.

I'm safe just sat here.

We hold others up, as they're learning to fly.
Patch up a wing, and take heed as we try
to get back on our feet,
And we do.

Eventually.

Brave face, head held high.
'Tits and teeth,' someone once said,
and that's what I think, when fear- filled dread-
stranglehold.

Take heed … I won't fall.
Guiding voices fill my mind.

If we live in the now, then surely we win:
an adventure once more;
an unwritten challenge.
Deep breath, step out-
plunge into life.
Own it.
And love it.
It's called: YOLO, they tell me.
No time for more strife.

Smile

Even the 'welcome mat' doesn't get its time to
feel its worth when visitors wipe their feet on the
pile.
The cups in the cupboard, and glasses- the good
stuff for guests- is waiting, albeit fretting these
lonely days will last.
And the children mourn their playdates and
seeing cousins in the flesh.
And I, their mother, can only quell and squash
these thoughts, which jibe and torment.
"Don't worry my pet, those days are back soon.
We will adventure those caves and mermaid
lagoons,
and visit soft play and party, party 'till dawn.
and our film nights, inside, will include
granddad, that's right!"

But under my breath, I shudder with fright.

My shattered, guilt-ridden mind conjures the
worst: I'm lying to hide the truth that we all
dread and fear.
Will these days turn to weeks, months or a year?
Will we ever be free and not tethered with fear?

No, says the hope, which is DEEP down inside.
One day at a time.
One hour, or half.
Take it easy, slow day and remember to smile.

Dane's Dyke

We marveled at your beauty.
We soaked up Sun's ray.
In awe, we smiled, as you scavenged,
yielding both dead and living treasures found
that day.

We embraced the quiet of our surroundings
blinding white stones deafened our sights.
But still there was this
feeling,
rising,
so tight...

I prayed that day.

You lit up as you played.
We knew the day would
Help to minds
as the world ripped our souls to shreds.

You paddled not too far from us,
climbed rocks and breathed in fresh sea air.
Adventuring Neptune's sea shore view
without a fear or care.

Buttercup Fields

That day was like many others we'd had before,
but not really.
We took you both for our daily walk:
The Westwood, and it was gorgeous!
It felt perfect. But in that blissful,
thirst - quenching moment
the sense of doom and fear crept in:
something would spoil a too perfect moment.

And it did.
But wait, imagine..

Lie back, close your eyes and breathe in the blue skies,
a lightly sketched-smudged- oil painting-
zig zag clouds high up,
framing the heavens above.
To the left of us a forest oozing with magic,
thick and thorny tempted every child looking for the big bad wolf,
or a mouse at least.

And others, quietly walked their dogs, musing their new lonely routines.
Some wore masks,

even though the magic of the forest told us to be
brave today.

You both play not far from safety-
the bookends- us-
holding it all together.

Even those big kids are out, the ones with the
huge remote- control airplanes.

NEEEAAAWWWWWWW

And then I see it; I drink in their yellow
glistening petals filling the rolling hills.
I still do like butter.
Cows moo not too far away.
A mother and her two girls casually,
        awkwardly,
wait their turn at the fallen tree trunk, which was
now the resident climbing frame hailed by all
the small humans mourning the closed
play-parks.

Bees buzzed and playpark.
commenced, out in the field.
No shirt and tie.
No swivel chairs.
No teas, coffees and pastries ordered to quench
this agenda.

But still, schedules were made; life goes on.

Then we heard it:
'He's fallen in the nettles!'

And, just like that, the 'no filter' moment of calm and serenity was over.

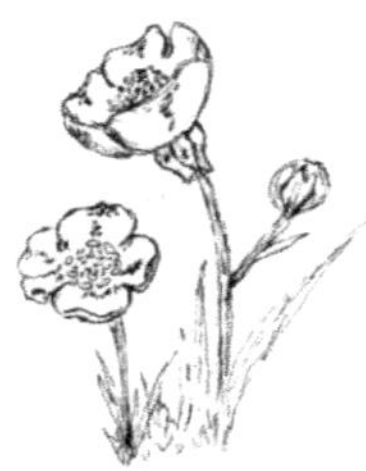

Pond Dipping

It was you that saw it first,
It didn't stay long- knowing its fate:
A boy with a net was never the right way to
venture.

Your eyes: keen and eager.
You shuddered with pride, awaiting what would
be the catch of the day.
The frog stared blankly.
Unflinchingly and clumsily it floundered at the
side of the murky waters, before making its
escape.

We, both shocked, marveled at it,
both beaming at our find.

The park was busy that sunny day.
Teenagers grouped together-
listening to their crap music, whilst scrolling
through mindless drivel on their phones.
Other young boys were there too
who were more prepared than us.
Big containers were held tightly,
chests puffed out and a determined focus:

to catch newts!

The guilt crept in.

Why didn't I think of the large container?
What else would I forget?

We stood, pondering,
figuring the best way to find a newt by listening
to the boys' advice.
And then, our time and snap shot of the past- a
fleeting time when we were a duo- was rudely
interrupted, as I ran off to retrieve your
side-kick:
our small master had ran off!

Back to: 'follow the leader' I play,
watching the invisible, yet strong twine
between us stretch out, tugging my heart
strings.

I didn't let you keep those fish that day.
And, you cried, but I stayed strong.
That lesson was a hard one son.
Some are my boy.

Scars and Scabs

How deep are these wounds?
We ask each other, most days.
And then the scabs heal. For a while.

Pick.
Pick.
Flick off the top,
and the wave of bile releases again.

Putrid grins,
devouring sins,
rage galore.

Time is a healer-
they say.
We say.

And, we tried.
Tried and tried and tried.
Cried. And cried and cried.
Patched up, both bandaged from head to toe
now.
Bloody, patched up cracks now open.

Time. Healing. Mending a broken heart.

And, still, love pours from those wounds we
share.
Forever, tattooed in my mind, and heart.
A kind of love, tattered and torn,
layers of hurt, embroiling it all.
We try to fix our broken wings.

Kintsugi repairs stronger they say,
but we've sold the gold that we now don't wear.

Holding hands
we let go.
Smiling,
makes us frown.
For now, time stands still.

Maybe we'll heal
through the pain;
through the fear;
through love, dear.

Take me off the map

Take me off the map for a while,
just for a day at least.
Until I can find which way is the way,
            if there's a way.
A closed sign; a board of Perspex or a mask.
To 'protect us,' they tell us.

I'm bored but full of energy; I'm a walking haze–
like my son with ALL of his questions.
We lie.
The parks are broken, the keys are lost, we say..

Until, months have passed and the other one aged two
announces:
'no more parks, no more beaches.'
And then the enormity of this global disaster nose
dives in my mind.

It's late now. Frazzled with numbers of deaths,
my body aches from cleaning each corner of the
kitchen floor with precision.
I've sprayed every handle and checked the doors are
locked,
Once
            Twice
                        Three for luck
I lie on my bed.
For a moment I float off away from it all- this surreal,
absurd reality of the:

'new norm'.

Top to toe, I feel around each curve and lump,
Stubble on my knees and hardened heels, crusted
with skin.
"I'll cut them tomorrow," I huff at my feet.
There's no chip.
No sign of entry.
No app will track me.

And where would I go if I went away?
Distant beaches spring to mind,
coves with mermaid lagoons to find.
Like scenes from a movie-
new home,
new name,
new buried treasure map in hand.

Today I'm just a 5

At the moment
I'm - ok.
Not high on love and the sweet smelling days of summer,
wine,
cold beers
ice pops,
At the moment.

Today I'm just a 5.
An average, grey underwear sort of day.
Maybe one up- lace trimmed pants.
Maybe I've brush my hair, washed my face?
Shaved?
Maybe.
Lip gloss, no - lip balm,
going for the natural look,
Scoff: CBA? Me?
Accessories on point, mostly-
chipped finger nails,
bitten a little after last week's debacle-
that text I saw.
Just don't really care right now.

At the moment.

Last week, I was a 7, for a bit.
Proud, curled hair,
painted my nails, went for a walk,
did a food shop without the clowns and clouds
raining down on my success.
Heart and head all normal.
No dizzy spell, without care:
A successful food shop,
thank you very much.
So at the moment I feel: fucking great.

I said this in the first session I had
over the phone with, Lisa.
New woman to listen as I lick my wounds.
Spilling my worries and cares and triggers all
over her pages of notes.
She decided she could work with me,
for me
charge me-
to change me.

Hope.
I have that.
At the moment.

Last year, maybe a 1.
And you, bridge high on a 0,
brought me to my knees.

Crashing down, I came.
You stayed; maybe at a 5.

The exploring.
The figuring, decluttering
my-
mind-
I lost you.
Well, me, before you.

At the moment I'm ok.

The chin hair, I quite like it.
And timetabled strife
knowing the next track in my Spotify life.
Regular systems,
I know where I stand.
I'll accessorize and plan and arrange to feel safe.
So I'll stay at a 5,
For now.
Standing still for a while.
No worrying, less thinking,

Today I feel fine.

The Second Song

We stepped in time with each other's' rhythm
that day.
That day.
Our daily walk-
Pilgrims.

The second song of the playlist you made,
however cheesy and utterly, oddly yet
Romantically out of character for you- made me
cry. And now I know the song my heart beats
out loudly.
You're still my one.
Look how far we've come.

And, that's why it hurts.
You know:
the thoughts and visions,
            flashes of boobs and thrusting,
zip up, and
                        rush out.
Drive off, quick-post-haste!
Probably in a haze, not looking back at
the mess you've made for us to clean up.

And what about the other songs meandering
through our lives, our hopes, dreams.
And the vows-
pull and push me to tempt and test if I can still
try.
Again, we'll try again.

Bridge high makes me dizzy I say,
as you pull me close.

But, with a small step across the uncertain void
I cockle in the heels I wear.
The fall is far. I know. He knows.
Falling is easy, you say, as you pull me closer,
so much closer.

An Ode to Youth

Gone are the days when we were carefree,
Alright in the morning,
And evening,
you and me.
Loving each day to day as we moseyed around,
Lives and limbs entwined and bound.

Yes, we argued, a love - intense -
Jealously overriding compassion and content.
Some old girl from the estate;
Same upbringing as bains.
A simple plan:
We loved, felt loved, and fumbled around like
the young.
Under a veil of Narnia once;
The willow tree, remember?
The blue moon looked on.
Tab kept us sweet,
doner meat and chips,
walking home after work
And all the smiles-
that smile.
Those eyes, green eyes to drown in.

Then we built this shitty love shack,

Red cherry paper on the wall.
And we partied- partied ‘till dawn.
We didn’t know what would end it all.
We didn’t care, curiosity satiated and fame
beckoned you,
I wasn’t there.
And then you were gone.

The dam of hardened, stifled emotion
    BrEaKs.
        Memories
escape and

Flood my heart.

It- just-really-hurts this time.
When I remember dumping potential in the bin.
No recycling back then, no stalking on
Facebook.
Just plain, eff off, I’m done.’
One chance.
First love.
You were gone.

Take me back to the days which were sweet,
young, wild and free.
Take me back to the ocean
play and sing for me.
In a mermaid lagoon, no Godfreys,

no Jaspers -
Just the sweet memories of Otis in the bathroom,
playing over
and over and over…

These arms of mine…

Can’t remember.
The past frittered away.
Too far from reach;
slovenly lyrics die at my feet.

And now I wander around seeking the lost boys
of the city,
with their grins, pouring gins and raiding
misery-obscured in the ghostly,
smoke filled void of lost youth.

Left to grow up in a mid-life haze of what ifs.

A celebration
A reunion
A chance of resolution
A hope
A chance to see and say:

The writing on the wall

Can't see the writing on the wall, behind the wall of a screen,
but each time I see her,
I only think of your name.
And in her eyes I see you,
before you rose to fame.

And then the claws dug into the trenches of a stolen love.
She waited patiently- longing for the pounce.
Claws sharpen, now her phone is at her side.
Bated breath, clinging to the hope
you will come home and abide.

Rising drumrolls of fear; an anxiety of chords;
a crescendo of the past,
playing until it hurts
turmoil breaks heart strings twang, and blast:
me.

History, revoked and rears it’s head.
A cacophony of base, drums, intermittent
screams from home invasion of fandom.
Unleashes this frozen tension melts and reveals
alternate realms and paths.

It flows, willingly through your veins- pacifying
the loyal fans.
Me.
Her.
And all in between - the hawks watch and wait.

And she too. Waits to release
the barrage of bile, as you enter your unexpected
ride home.
And you know

We all know.

Home. The little one sleeps, unbeknown to the
shitty lessons in love being taught beneath the
floor of his cocoon.
Silent, snide remarks and a barrage of
embryonic questions, exploding comfortably
again into a retake of the Alien birth scene:
cheap fx, gore and all, laden out for all to bear
witness across the kitchen, the hall:
staining the home with the stench of the unjust
froth of:
nothing.

And maybe those days, or moments of calm:
suppressed under totalitarian control, creep into
your life and twist the cogs to seize and evoke
dreams of the past.

Hauntingly beautiful ghost sightings through the crowds bemuse you and entice.

We all want summat like that.

Evacuating resentment for a while.
Move the benchmark a tad further.
Behaving, pacifying- we all hold up the cracked tiles falling down- which cover the escape route.
You. Will. Conform.
You. Will. Be good.
You. Will. Stay.
Everything is okay.

Until,
the bath falls through the ceiling.

Fossil Hunting

It's funny how love erupts,
like a volcano spilling a surging heat of lust,
dressed as love.
Rushes, spews out a river of lava.
Penetrating, eradicating innocent lives.
Taken by surprise- no warning- no sign. Dictated
trials of destruction.
Destroying all in its path.

First: raging,stirring, passionate.
And then one day-
Nothing.
Hardened, molten lava capturing a moment in
time,
creating new forms which binds
Stoney rocks form.
Tough.
Hardened casing.
Hardened centre.

But people forget, pain subsides and
Landslide into the past.
Seeing decadent skies,
Smoke gets in our eyes.
Blinding and comprising our time.

And life, oh life,
spanning decades goes by.

We crack open what was there:
Nothing.

Fragile, unforgettable moments,
entwined, like lovers at sunrise:
Dissipated.
Just like that.
Gone.

But still I search.

Sediments must be somewhere hidden in the past.
Fog filled dance floors arise, in my mind's eye
And you- my first- are there to catch my smile.

Fossil hunting.
Fossil finding.
Fossil love never dies.

Secrets of Yours

Secrets stashed for rainy days
Aren't kept secret forever.
But I kept some, for you-
like some sacred treasure.
A Ronson lighter, still in its original packaging;
Your brother, a proud solider, son- to mother-
his hand writing so neat, telling tales from war.
The scars, small meals and wounds to heal.
And, of course, the wish to be back home
Even us everyday soldiers still yearn to return
home.

And, I wandering around your house that day,
Whilst you, locked away in the home,
Wondered why you'd lived alone so many years.
No husband to share a secret, a smile
A love and children.
No pet to keep you company and listen to your
inner world,
Tall tales of Bingo,
Or shopping for Handbags with Mo.

we then reached your bedroom,
The drawers and shoe boxes,

Full to the brim,
We unpicked your life
And then it sunk in,
Some memories we erased,
Some we salvaged and saved,
Included the stash of the love that he gave.

Butcher Bill.
Secret love letters, spanning decades of deceit,
For his wife (name unknown) never knew how he wished,
That he could be with you,
And live a simple life,
Visiting the beach;
Not with his wife.
Valentines, Christmases, love filed postcards received
And all of this unknown, unspoken of…
Until after, when we grieved.

I looked at his photo.
I took in his small smile.
Unfurling, summoning my own lost loves for a while.

I sent you that photo,
Maybe it would help you to stay,
In the arms of our world, so we could regain,

The lost time of the months that we couldn't visit
you.
But instead, two weeks later- on the floor
They found you.

We laid you to rest,
We cried,
And I smiled.
I prayed that he'd find you,
I wished that you'd reunite.
Maybe up above you'll find love,
Secretly kepping him hidden tight,
out of sight.

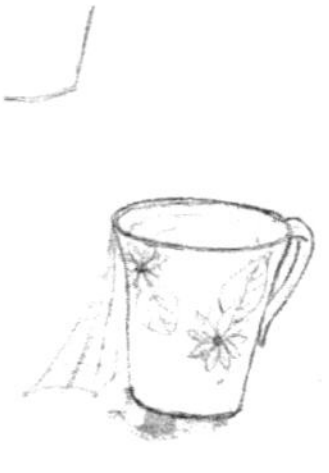

The Mothership

Today I returned to the Mothership.
My copied key (just in case) tucked safely in my pocket.
I knew how quiet the world would be
when I got there.

I slipped inside.
Wry smile- small suitcase in hand.
The smell hits: home.

Thirty years of memories peacefully,
pounce at me, gently like the butterflies we were told not to catch.

Trinkets of yours, photos both new and old, bits and bobs here and there:
Home.
Some stuff still sat there on the bottom stair,
waiting for someone to take it upstairs.
I do.

The smallest room now filled with worn, precious, retro finds-
Barbie's caravan is the new favourite amongst the grandkids.
And the dolls, still stare.
Snide, RBF faces, with their badly hacked hair;
probably still pissed that their locks had been bluntly chopped,
blunt scissors in the grubby hands of the

ever-confident petulant know-it-all: me.

I open the curtains.
The south facing garden there still.
Seagulls circling above.
I close my eyes and absorb those garden camping nights with friends-
remembering how every sound felt like the end of our lives was near.
It was all for love, wasn't it?

Pushing open the window-
to fall, or fly?
Seagulls scream out.
As- I – jump out to be Wendy once again.
Flying past the pear tree, grape vine, even lettuce you grow now.
Landing gracefully I settle at the shed door.
Ajar, I slink in,
not too near the motorbike,
he'd only moan.
It's not like the days when we rode down the garden, one by one,
each of us taking turns to greet daddy coming home from work.
The same smell engulfs me- oily, workman-type smell,
Tools stacked, and boxes with this and that:
your magic tricks ready at hand to come and fix whatever we need.
Whenever we need you:
Home.

I sit on the swing.
Youth swoops by: hedgehog hunts in the long grasses
next door,
chasing rabbits, and dogs...
then the pounding music from loud speakers hits me.
Even the decks have moved out.

I lock up, close the gate behind me,
and a reel of the past replays:
denim jacket, young lovers sigh.
"You're a peach you know," he'd say.
I'd blush, we kissed.
I drink it all in-
knowing that I'd have to drive back to the landfill
home-
abruptly left,
unfinished jigsaw,
mad mum strife and life to revive.
The kids would miss me, I think.

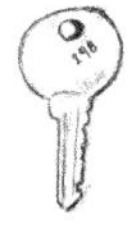

Sing a New Song

Warm rays held us tight.
Sun rays smiled down cutting through
our burden and strife.
Preparing, re-arranging.
To sell up and leave.
The decision was made.

The kids played- messing up each orchestrated
room as we chartered these furniture filled
rooms, hiding the troubles we had endured,
for so long now.
Too long.
Until the photographer arrived.
Chirpy, polite, shirt and tie sort of guy.

Nice. He was, nice,
if you know what I mean.
Capturing the:
'perfect home for a growing family.'
"Detached, linked detached?"

Maybe some other family would make use of it.
Without the harsh crash-landing from grace,
perhaps?

And as I, and you, wandered around memory
embalmed rooms- stuffing the bits and bobs into
bags:
The façade: a fabricated, parfait Pintrest picture
– perfection.
Smirking: the poly-filled holes in doors and
walls watched on: they knew.
The kids paraded around, showing off their
play-fighting skills as the untarnished
twenty-something guy- with his lenses, tripod,
found the right angles of sale.

When he left, it felt
wrong.

You left: therapy calls- setting time set aside to
bandage the decades of damage residing in the
heat of your heart and burn scars.
I – the collateral damage – just sobbed.

Sobbed and sobbed, until there was a knock at
the door.
Chiquittia played on the radio, Alexa knew-
know it all, interfering bitch.
And you did too- flowers in hand, my mate,
comrade, my rock-
held me so tight and sponged my pain away.
A coffee; a chat.

And then back to mummying making jacket
potatoes for tea.

And that's that: the for sale sign sang:
"you'll be dancing once a again and the pain will
end
Sing a new song Chiquitita."

You 'left' again.

The evening sun was so gorgeous that evening-
You must remember it?
I bet it made you sweat your balls off biking all that way.

Rucksack- filled with normal essentials this time: clothes, cosmetics, chargers etc
Unlike the first frantic attempt leaving with a suitcase full of books.
And a sink full of the blood for me to clean up.

Self harm – it's a funny thing. All forms of it we've met head on.
Panic attack, post-haste, a discombobulating haze.
Compounding you in the lies which became the flies circling the fresh corpse of our dying marriage.

"And only four weeks after the wedding?"

Therapists, I fucking love them; loath them all in one.

“And six weeks pregnant? Honeymoon baby?”
she nods and furrows her brow slightly. Write a
few notes, or draws a stick man- who knows?

We are spilling my baggage onto her pages.
Each note, ink-smudged with the frantic
scribbles- clogging me,
choking me.
Releasing the pent up rage I’ve kept in:
exorcizing my grief, analysing why I let him in.
Dissecting my wounds of the delightful decades
of my frazzled mind, and yet,
I still manage a joke or two.
“That’s just a coping mechanism.”
(Yeah, no shit Sherlock.)

I digress. Where was I?
Oh, the sun.. of course- everything is sunny
when you’re comfortably numb.
Looking out the window I see you bike off.
Surrounded by the perfect little 1960s estate,
blossom trees set free their bloom as if they are
celebrating my sadness, and the hauntingly
beautiful flashes of our wedding day taunt me.

Boys at my side we look out-
“He’ll be back in the morning, love.”

Too tired to think.

Too tired to cry.
Too tired to feel.

And then the bedtime story is upon us.
My thespian voice erodes the sadness,
Terrible accents arise,
they laugh;
I cry.

Rise.

As I sit in my room and wail, 'why me?'
Leaning out of my window, I curse people, quite pathetically.
Of course, COVID has bashed me– again- and thrown away the key.
Not today. Really? Why today? And then I rise, make some tea.

Into my bedroom I go; still serving food at the door.
But in this invisible snare which holds me, I ponder.
Alone.
Magazines- not read- laden out on the bed, I shred,
tear out pages and pages and pages, like a frenzied, angry and puzzled weirdo.
What's next?

And then, by Jove- PING! Images mutated.
My new life was there, waiting patiently on pages.
To carve and compile, create and conceive it.
I stared in awe as it danced out its song.
This dream-like vision edged towards me.

Half amazed; half scared- I let it commence.

Images of oceans and adventures await,
Freedom with friends, fresh air on my face.
Muted, calms tones for a home that I'll make.
It warmed me through, and into my soul
and now I see it.

I CAN rise again.
I CAN un-leash my potential- unearth my lost career.
I CAN rise to just, be.

You see, this year, is quite different from the seventeen days of yore.
A divorce.
It's happening.
Years of pain: "I can't take no more."
Lies, deceit, adultery, addiction- where does it end?

Is love enough? Sacred oaths, like magical fairy wedding day dust-
now gather, and clog up where there isn't chipping, flaking rust.
Our children don't know, yet; we can't carry on and pretend.
As we pack their belongings, like it's game: they don't know the end.

Then one day I saw these words extend out their
lips to my ears, whispering gently:
"When someone shows you who they are the
first time, believe who they are."

To her, I owe my freedom.
"still I rise."

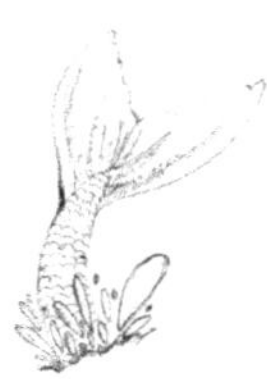

For Sale.

Home is up for sale.
Bitter sadness erodes me.
Time to say goodbye.

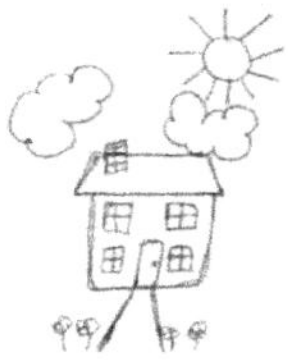

www.ingramcontent.com/pod-product-compliance
Lightning Source LLC
Chambersburg PA
CBHW051736130826
49812CB00033B/889
9789357210577